My Family
Mi Familia

My Cousins
Mis primos

Emily Sebastian

PowerKiDS press & **Editorial Bue**

New York

Published in 2011 by The Rosen Publishing Group, Inc.
29 East 21st Street, New York, NY 10010

Copyright © 2011 by The Rosen Publishing Group, Inc.

First Edition

Editor: Amelie von Zumbusch
Book Design: Ashley Burrell

Photo Researcher: Brian Garvey
Spanish Translation: Eduardo Alamán

Photo Credits: Cover, pp. 5, 6, 11 (cousin) © www.iStockphoto.com/Aldo Murillo; pp. 8–9, 11 (dad, mom, aunt), 16, 18–19 Shutterstock.com; p. 11 (brother) © www.iStockphoto.com/ Ekaterina Monakhova; p. 11 (sister) © www.iStockphoto.com/quavondo; p. 11 (uncle) © www. iStockphoto.com/asiseeit; p. 11 (grandfather) © www.iStockphoto.com/Juanmonino; p. 11 (grandmother) © www.iStockphoto.com/Elena Ray; p. 12–13 © www.iStockphoto.com/heidijpix; p. 15 © www.iStockphoto.com/Eileen Hart; p. 21 Terry Vine/Getty Images; p. 22 Hill Street Studios/Getty Images.

Library of Congress Cataloging-in-Publication Data

Sebastian, Emily.
  My cousins = Mis primos / Emily Sebastian — 1st ed.
      p. cm. — (My family = Mi familia)
  Includes index.
  ISBN 978-1-4488-0720-8 (library binding)
  1. Cousins—Juvenile literature. I. Title.
  HQ759.97.S33 2011
  306.87—dc22
                                        2010009427

Manufactured in the United States of America

CPSIA Compliance Information: Batch #WS10PK: For Further Information contact Rosen Publishing, New York, New York at 1-800-237-9932

Web Sites: Due to the changing nature of Internet links, PowerKids Press and Editorial Buenas Letras have developed an online list of Web sites related to the subject of this book. This site is updated regularly. Please use this link to access the list: www.powerkidslinks.com/family/cousin/

Contents / Contenido

Cousins 4

A Family Tree 10

Fun with Cousins.............................12

Words to Know 24

Index 24

Primos y primas 4

El árbol genealógico 10

Disfrutando con tus primos.................12

Palabras que debes saber...................24

Índice 24

Cousins in Latin American families are close. They like spending time together.

En las familias de Latinoamérica los primos son muy cercanos. A los primos les gusta pasar tiempo juntos.

5

Mateo's mom and Sam's mom are sisters. This makes Mateo and Sam cousins.

La mamá de Mateo y la mamá de Sam son hermanas. Por eso, Mateo y Sam son primos.

Laura and David are cousins, too. Their dads are brothers.

Laura y David también son primos. Sus papás son hermanos.

As you can see on this **family tree**, cousins have the same grandparents.

Como puedes ver en este **árbol genealógico**, los primos tienen los mismos abuelos.

Family Tree / Árbol Genealógico

Grandfather / Abuelo

Grandmother / Abuela

Uncle / Tío

Aunt / Tía

Dad / Papá

Mom / Mamá

Cousin / Primo

Brother / Hermano

Sister / Hermana

Martín has six cousins. Some kids have no cousins, while others have many.

Martín tiene seis primos. Algunos chicos no tienen primos. Otros tienen muchos primos.

Brianna lives next door to her cousins. They see one another often.

Brianna vive junto a la casa de sus primos. Brianna y sus primos se ven con mucha frecuencia.

Isabel's cousins live in Puerto Rico. She talks to them often on the phone.

Los primos de Isabel viven en Puerto Rico. Isabel habla con ellos por teléfono.

These cousins are visiting their grandmother in Mexico. They went to the beach there!

Estos primos están visitando a su abuela en México. ¡Allí, fueron a la playa!

Ana's cousins came to her birthday party. Cousins make birthdays extra fun!

Todos los primos de Ana fueron a su fiesta de cumpleaños. ¡Los primos hacen los cumpleaños muy divertidos!

Family **reunions** are great times to have fun with your cousins.

Las **reuniones** familiares son una buena oportunidad para divertirte con tus primos.

Words to Know /
Palabras que debes saber

family tree (FAM-lee TREE) A chart that shows the members of a family.

reunions (ree-YOON-yunz) The coming together of families, friends, or other groups of people.

árbol genealógico (el) Una tabla en la que se muestra a los miembros de una familia.

reuniones (las) Cuando las personas se juntan.

<table>
<tr><td>

Index

</td><td>

Índice

</td></tr>
</table>

Index

B

birthday party, 20

F

family tree, 10

G

grandparents, 10

R

reunions, 23

Índice

A

abuelos, 10

árbol genealógico, 10

F

fiesta de cumpleaños, 20

R

reuniones, 23